By Laura Williams
Translated by Jaspreet Kaur

© 2022 Williams Books
1 rue de l'église, 91430 Igny
Dépôt légal : Décembre 2022
ISBN 978-2-494614-55-0
Imprimé à la demande par Amazon
Loi n° 49-956 du 16 juillet 1949 sur les publications destinées à la jeunesse

ਸੇਬ

[seb] – apple

ਆਵੇਕੈਡੋ

[avocado] – avocado

केला

[kela] – banana

ਫਲੀਆਂ

[phaliyaan] – beans

ਪੱਤਾਗੋਭੀ

[pataagobhi] – cabbage

ਗਾਜਰ

[gaajar] – carrot

ਮਿਰਚ

[mirach] – chilli

ਮੱਕੀ

[makki] – corn

ਖੀਰਾ

[kheera] – cucumber

ਬੈਂਗਨ

[baingan] – eggplant

ਲਸਣ

[lasan] – garlic

ਅਦਰਕ

[adarak] – ginger

ਹਰੀਆਂ ਫਲੀਆਂ

[hariaan phaliyaan] – green beans

ਅਮਰੂਦ

[amrood] – guava

ਨਿੰਬੂ

[nimbu] - lemon

ਅੰਬ

[amb] – mango

ਖੁੰਭ

[khubh] - mushroom

ਪਿਆਜ਼

[pyaaj] – onion

ਸੰਤਰਾ

[santra] – orange

ਪਪੀਤਾ

[papita] – papaya

ਜਾਨੂਨੀ ਫਲ

[janooni phal] – passion fruit

ਮੁੰਗਫਲੀ

[mungphali] - peanut

ਮਟਰ

[matter] – peas

ਅਨਾਨਾਸ

[anaanaas] – pineapple

ਆਲੂ

[aaloo] – potato

ਪੇਠਾ

[pettha] – pumpkin

ਚੌਲ

[chaul] – rice

ਸੋਇਆ

[soya] – soy

पालक

[paalak] – spinach

ਗੰਨਾ

[ganna] – sugar cane

ਮਿਠਾ ਆਲੂ

[mitthaa aaloo] – sweet potato

ਟਮਾਟਰ

[ttamaattar] - tomato

ਤਰਬੂਜ

[tarbooj] – watermelon

कनक

[kanak] – wheat

Thank you

Thank you for purchasing "Punjabi-English Words for Toddlers"! Your support means a lot to me, and I hope you and your child enjoy these books.

If you have a moment, I would greatly appreciate it if you could leave a review on Amazon. Your feedback will help me improve future editions of the series and create more resources for bilingual children.

Thank you again for your support. You can access the reviews on Amazon by scanning the QR code below or by visiting the link below:

https://www.amazon.com/review/create-review?&asin=2494614554

Thank you for helping me continue my work as a language teacher and translator. Your support is greatly appreciated!

In the same collection